"Executive Farm"
A Leadership Fable

By Victor Prince

Dedication

To Uncle Jerry and Uncle Norton.
Your farms were more productive
than you ever knew.

Chapter 1
"A Secret Retreat"

The private jet touched down at a small rural airstrip. Once it taxied to the only building in sight, the runway lights shut off. The sun was setting. A shuttle bus idled nearby, its air conditioner running in the warm summer evening. Once the last passenger climbed aboard and stowed his bags, the driver swung the door shut and slowly pulled off.

A tall, thin woman in a smart white pantsuit stood at the front of the aisle and turned to talk to the passengers. "I hope everyone enjoyed the flight. It will be about twenty to thirty minutes until we get to our destination, so make yourselves comfortable. I see you all staring at your phones. You won't find much signal here, but you will have access to a landline when we arrive. I'll get back up as we near our destination and share the rest of the details I know you are eager to hear."

Six of the eight passengers traded quick, knowing glances and suppressed smug smiles as they put their mobile phones away. This woman, Riordan, was obviously relishing the 'big reveal' she had in store for them. The real surprise, however, was that these six co-conspirators had secretly pieced together the destination through creative team detective work over the last few weeks.

Rewind to a few weeks before. The seventh passenger on the bus, a CEO named Nordy, introduced Riordan to his team of six direct reports as an executive coach he hired. "Each of you is an A-plus player in your field," Nordy started, "but for some reason, we are only a B-minus team together. As Team Leader, I take responsibility for that and have asked Riordan to coach me to become a better leader. She is going to start by interviewing each of you to help understand where I can provide better leadership."

After one-on-one meetings with everyone, Riordan reported back the insights from the interviews at the weekly staff meeting with Nordy and his direct reports. Riordan kept the feedback anonymous, as she promised, but she didn't hold any punches. While all the criticism was worded constructively, it was still brutal.

Hearing the feedback out loud made everyone realize they were a lot more blunt and open with her than they had intended to be...or even remembered being. Everyone snuck glances at Nordy when a particularly harsh piece of feedback they shared came out.

After a seeming eternity, Riordan ended with a summary and proposal. "I've done these types of assessments for years. This is the most troubling I've ever seen. You are behaving like a group of competitors, not a team of colleagues. You hold back information from each other. You focus more on individual credit than team results. When a problem arises, you look for blame instead of solutions. You are too competitive to offer help to each other and too territorial to accept it. You urgently need to change these behavior patterns and I know your best path to do that. Your annual executive retreat is coming up in a few weeks. I know the place that will help you gel as a team. I can take care of all the arrangements. My only condition is that you let me plan it in secret."

Nordy looked around at six other faces all looking back at him. He was normally stoic, but after an uncharacteristic long gap of silence, something changed in his face. He pushed back his chair dramatically, stood and said in a raised voice, "This is not acceptable!" Nordy seemed as close to angry as they had ever seen. The report Riordan had just delivered was a punch in the gut to him. He had taken it quietly but it had obviously hit a nerve.

After a moment, Nordy sat back down and smiled as his usual self and continued. "You all know I don't like surprises. But I really, really hate underperforming. And something obviously needs to change. As long as you can promise nobody gets hurt, I'm game for anything for our retreat, Riordan." He stood up again and walked to the door. "Especially if I can get at least one round of golf in," he said with a smile and winked as he walked out.

Everyone nervously smiled back and gestured at Nordy as he left. They had plenty of criticisms of their boss, but getting flustered like that was not one of them. Riordan broke the silence. "So I'll take that as the OK to start planning your retreat. Meeting adjourned," she said as she walked out as well.

If Riordan had not assumed the authority to adjourn their meeting, maybe the rest of the people in that room would not have felt so peeved at her. They were all stung that she had just told their boss all the harsh criticisms they had shared with her. They also resented the fact that she had assumed their consent for her to take over their retreat plans.

They took advantage of having the room to themselves to debrief on what just happened. They decided they would not try to overturn the de facto OK to have Riordan plan their retreat.

Nordy's pride was hurt in a way they had never seen and they didn't want to pick at that wound. But they did agree to resist. Their resistance wasn't going to be a protest; it was going to be an inquest. No matter what, they decided Riordan wouldn't be able to surprise them. They would do whatever they had to do to figure out the secret location Riordan was planning.

Over the next few weeks, Lloyd, the Chief Information Officer, pulled all the emails Riordan had ever sent or received through the company email system. Nora, the Chief Financial Officer, scoured every expense report Riordan submitted. Jerry, Chief Operating Officer, called in some favors from an old Navy buddy now working at the FAA to alert him to any private jet flight plans for those dates from their airport. Eva, the Chief Human Capital Officer, had her HR team shake all the trees to figure out where this 'coach' Riordan had staged executive retreats before. Joanne, the General Counsel, even looked into the criminal code to see where "surprise destination" could be equated to kidnapping if they had to get leverage over Riordan. Maro, the Chief Marketing Officer, didn't have a specific angle to add but offered to coordinate all the individual efforts.

They met secretly over breakfast twice a week to review what they had learned. Hotel reservations. Charter plane flight plans. Emailed itineraries. After three weeks of work, they had pieced it together. They figured out they were headed to a small airfield in Chanute, Minnesota.

The only thing in Chanute, Minnesota was a golf resort on a private lake with a rare Michelin-star restaurant and an exclusive golf course nearby. Their concern turned to happiness. They even downloaded the menu of the restaurant and figured out what they were going to order each night. They had all been looking forward to their original planned resort destination, but they had been there before and were excited to go somewhere new. The "surprise" aspect of the trip had been stressful, but they were all glad how it was turning out.

The shuttle bus slowed, turned and then stopped. The interior lights came on and Riordan got up again to talk. "Welcome to your destination."

Six pairs of eyes darted to meet each other. They all suppressed smug smiles again.

"Actually, I know you are not surprised," Riordan added. "I want to commend you all for figuring out our secret destination. The purpose of making the destination secret was to challenge you to work together to figure it out. I planted those pieces of the puzzle across all of your departments that could only be solved if you collaborated."

Six heads cocked back and looked at each other with puzzled smiles.

"Now think if you collaborated as much in your real work," Riordan continued. "How many of the problems you told me about in our interviews could have been solved if you cooperated instead of relying on Nordy to referee every conflict between you? How many of the problems arose because you compete instead of cooperate? What problems could you solve together that you can't solve individually? Why did you work together so well on this? Was it because you were all focused on the same common enemy? Why can't you do that with other company-wide problems?"

The bus door swung open on Riordan's cue: "So yes, you did figure out our destination. Congratulations. Welcome to Chanute, Minnesota." A burst of humid, pungent air rushed in.

"Whoa. What is that smell?" someone said.

Riordan answered, "Yes, we are in Chanute, but that fancy resort you identified is a few miles down the road. We are at a small dairy farm. That smell is fresh country air perfumed with cow manure. Let's get you inside, fed and comfortable, because this is where you are having your retreat."

Chapter 2
The Michelline Meal

Eight people in business-casual clothes walked toward an old farmhouse, struggling with their luggage rollers on the gravel driveway. Riordan led the group to a door that opened to a kitchen. A cat scurried from under the porch when the first dress shoe hit the creaky wooden step.

Riordan flipped on the kitchen light and explained the logistics. "There are two bedrooms upstairs, each with two single beds. I suggest Nora, Eva, Maro and Joanne take those. Lloyd and Jerry, there is a couch in the living room and an aero bed in the dining room. You two figure it out. Nordy, since you are the boss, I've got you in the one single bedroom down on this floor. There is one bathroom upstairs and one down here, right off the kitchen. Why don't you all unpack and then come back down for dinner. Dinner is in the crock-pot and fridge with instructions on how to prepare it. I'm going to stay at the motel in town with the bus driver and the pilots. I'll see you all at five a.m. tomorrow and explain the plan for the rest of our retreat. Good night." With that, Riordan slipped out and boarded the bus, which immediately started backing out the driveway. Her audience was too discombobulated to stop her.

The group of seven well-dressed city folks looked at each other with a sense of mild silent shock.

"Whiskey Tango Foxtrot?" Jerry said to break the ice, using a Navy saying he learned on his first submarine patrol. It took the rest of the group a second to decode that, and when they did they all started laughing nervously.

"OK team, I'm not sure what I've gotten us into, but the one thing I do know is that I'm starving," Nordy said. "How about we settle in and meet back here in the kitchen in fifteen minutes?"

Everyone agreed and found their assigned corner of the old house. While old, the house was Pine-Sol clean and well maintained and had a rustic charm to it. The first thing they did was turn on the window air conditioning units. As soon as the third one flipped on, the house went completely dark—country dark, without any streetlights backlighting the house. Then, one by one, seven iPhones-turned-flashlights started moving through the pitch black like fireflies. Nordy somehow found the breaker box by the refrigerator and got the power back on.

Their first crisis solved, the gang started pulling out dishes from the fridge, each with a Post-It note attached with elaborate but undecipherable handwritten instructions on how to warm them in the microwave and oven. The main dish was some sort of chicken casserole. The side dishes were au-gratin potatoes and green beans. Dessert was a Jell-O mold with marshmallows and whipped cream layered in. Large urns of iced tea and milk were the only beverages visible in the fridge.

The shock had started to wear off and the thought of this reality-TV-worthy stunt now extending to their hunger made their situation more real. Nordy sensed the tension and broke it with a joke. "Not quite like the first meal we had at our retreat at the Greenbrier last year, is it? How bad can it be?" With that, Nordy took a forkful of potatoes and gave an approving grin as he swallowed.

They sat around the table in the kitchen and Nordy served them. "It's the least I can do for getting us into this. And it gets me out of cleanup duty," he said with a wink.

A few minutes into the meal, Lloyd decided to address the elephant in the room. "Nordy, we're sorry we didn't tell you we figured out Chanute as the secret location. We were all worried about going somewhere secret, so yes, we did figure it out as Riordan said. And yes, it was a fun experience to piece it together as a team and it taught us to work together better. That said, there was a downside in doing that. I knew exactly what I was going to order off the menu for the next four days. And this ain't it."

Everyone laughed and that opened a floodgate of jokes comparing the food they were eating now to the food they had planned to eat and the food they'd had at past retreats. All the built-up nervous energy was released, as everyone tried to top everyone else with their jokes. The jokes got pretty raucous and a few laughed so hard they came to tears.

As the energy started dying down and the food was all picked over, Nordy asked everyone to raise their glasses for a toast.

"As executives, we work hard and we get paid well for that work. If we want to enjoy the finer things in life as a reward for that work, more power to us. Many times, however, senior executives can lose touch with the people who enable them to have such good lives—their customers. I've sensed that we have lost touch with our customers. We have talked about things we are going to do as senior leaders to keep ourselves and teams connected to our customers at our last three retreats. But while we remember the meals we had at each of those, we've forgotten to carry through with the commitments we made there. I wanted to spend the weekend living in the shoes of our customers, so I chose this location, Riordan didn't. This house belongs to a family who is one of our best customers. It is not unlike the homes of thousands of our customers."

Nordy made a point to make eye contact with each person and continued, "In fact, this home belongs to my brother Stan and his wife Michelle. Michelle made this meal we just ate after working all day at her job in a window factory, coming home to feed herself and her husband, and then staying up late to make this extra meal. So I will thank Michelle profusely for you all next time I see her, and I'll see you at five a.m. right here. Good night."

Nordy walked off to his bedroom and shut his door, leaving six stunned faces behind.

Chapter 3
The Golf Trips

"Good morning, Nora," Nordy said as his first breakfast guest appeared. It was before five a.m., but he already had coffee brewing, eggs frying, toast toasting and the kitchen table set. Other lights turned on and people started shuffling into the kitchen. "What can I make you?" Nordy said as he greeted each with a smile.

By five, everyone was down in the kitchen as requested, punctual even on a retreat. Nordy guided them all to seats at the table.

"I owe you an apology and an explanation," Nordy said. "First, I've erased last night from my memory. If there are any apologies needed, they are only from me to you for setting you up. I did it to make it a point. It was unfair but I trust you all will eventually understand and forgive me."

"Second," Nordy continued, "Riordan isn't coming back. She is an old friend of mine who played a role I asked her to. The one thing I do give you my word on is that she hasn't, and won't ever, tell me the names of who gave specific feedback. None of the feedback I heard angered or surprised me, so when I raised my voice at that meeting, it was just part of the act Riordan and I were putting on.

"Third, I have to confess something else. Those exotic 'golf trip' weekends you think I take every month have actually been trips to this farm. This is the farm where I grew up. When I left for college, my brother stayed to keep the farm going with our parents. I come back here one weekend a month to give my brother and his wife a break. Dairy farmers work seven days a week, fifty-two weeks a year. No weekends, no holidays. Cows have to get milked morning and night. My brother and sister-in-law don't have any kids or other relatives to relieve them and that is the only form of help they will take from me. I find this work helps me too. It keeps me grounded, reminds me what 'hard work' is, clears my mind and relaxes me. As fellow high-pressure corporate executives, I thought it would do the same for you. That's why we are all here."

Eva, the Chief Human Capital Officer, looked around to the rest of her colleagues and said,

"Nordy, first, I want to apologize for the whole team for our comments about our meal last night. We all feel terrible. After you went to bed, we stayed at this table for two and a half hours talking about the issues you raised about us losing touch with our customers. We ended up sharing our own stories about what we were like before we got on these executive fast-tracks. We all agree it was an eye-opening discussion. As the 'HR' person, I've been empowered by my colleagues to say that. I think I am also speaking for the whole team when I say we are thrown off by this whole experience, but we trust you, and we will follow your lead."

Nordy gave them a look they hadn't seen in a long time. "Thanks for that, Eva and all. That means a lot to me. It really does."

"We do have one question," Maro, the Chief Marketing Officer, chirped in. "Please tell us your brother and his wife went somewhere fun this weekend to make us feel better about the hard work I think we are about to experience."

Nordy shook his head. "Oh, my brother and his wife didn't get this weekend off. They are working their neighbor's farm down the road."

Multiple loud cow moos cut him off as the sunrise started to hit the window.

"Whoa. We are running way too late. We really gotta go. The cows can't wait any longer," Nordy said as he glanced at his watch. "Our work clothes and boots are in those labeled boxes in the corner. Let's get suited up and on the porch as quickly as possible."

Chapter 4
Coax, Command, Commiserate

The group gathered on the porch and admired the sunrise. They wore identical uniforms with denim overalls tucked into tall rubber boots. They walked awkwardly across the driveway to the cinderblock building attached to the red barn.

Nordy opened the door to the building and ushered them in. "Welcome to the dairy parlor. Keep your hands inside the vehicle at all times and don't touch any of the animals." he said with a smile. Once inside, they crowded around the big milk tank that dominated the entry room and Nordy gave a short speech. "I obviously know what is about to happen because I have been doing this for decades. This afternoon you are going to do this yourselves. So take notes, keep your head on a swivel to help out when I ask, and stay out of the way otherwise."

With that, Nordy flipped on a loud compressor and opened the door to another room with a U-shaped raised tier floor waist-high around it. He pulled himself up to the upper tier, closed a metal gate behind him, and then grabbed the handle to a large door. "Let the show begin." He smiled as he swung the door open and six 1300 lb (600 kg) black and white spotted Holstein cows ambled their way in and gently assumed their spots in the stanchions in order.

As soon as the sixth cow entered, Nordy closed the door and jumped back down to floor level to a garbage can at the far side of the parlor. He opened it, scooped a huge serving of grain and poured it in a bucket by the first cow. He repeated that for each of the cows. Then he went to cow number one with a bucket and sponges and cleaned off its udders as it contently chewed its grain meal. (He must have prepped this soapy solution before breakfast, they all noted.) He then pulled a loud octopus-looking contraption off a hook by the cow's head, flipped it upside-down and carefully put a milking vacuum on each of the four cow teats. He checked that each one was working by seeing the milk bubbling uphill to the overhead pipes back to the bulk tank in the anteroom.

After he repeated the process for each cow, he had a bit of downtime. He gathered his spectators back to the anteroom around the bulk tank.

"It takes a few minutes for each milking session to complete. In a moment I am going to open the exit door and let these cows out and open the other door to let the next set it. The milking process is exactly the same. Clean cow, milk cow, clean cow. The art comes in with the cows themselves. They bring different energy each time. The same cows always come in the first chute and always act the same. They have some sort of hierarchy that they figure out amongst themselves. The next batches are more mixed, as they joust for order to get to the grain. I'll never know what goes on between them, but I've learned to read the energy each batch brings. Every time I open that door, I have to figure out the energy my hundred and seventy-pound body needs to project to direct the eight thousand pounds of cow that I just let into my space. Sometimes I need to coax. Sometimes I need to command. Sometimes I need to commiserate. Whatever I do, I have figured out that I have to do it with calm, quiet confidence because that is the one thing they always need from their leader. I let that chute of cows out and let in the next. Each milking is five sets of cows and I get slightly better at milking after each. Speaking of which, it sounds like chute two is ready. Let's get back in there. I hope you are taking notes."

Four more milkings ensued and the spectators increasingly got involved as they learned the process. By the last chute, everyone was helping and Nordy was more of a supporting cast member than Lead Actor.

When the last chute of cows left, everyone cheered and high-fived. They were all goal-oriented professionals who had just met a new goal they never knew existed. A high of endorphins rushed through them.

Nordy smiled and fist-bumped each of them. Then he said, "If you wondered why you all are wearing those tall rubber boots, you are about to find out. Milking is hard work. Post-milking is dirty work." He grabbed a shovel and pulled himself up to the milking tier. "Like every productive thing in life, milk has a by-product. And I am going to show you how we handle it."

Nordy then pushed and shoveled countless pounds of manure out of the door into a manure-spreader wagon. He hosed off the rest down a drain. It became clear why the boots he wore were almost up to his knees, as he was often ankle-deep in manure.

Nordy finished pushing and pitching manure as everyone watched, some holding their noses. "If I had not grown up doing this, I would probably think shoveling ankle-deep animal waste was about the most disgusting thing anyone could do. But I see shoveling manure as crucial work that someone has to do to make the milk and ice cream we all love. Many times executives underappreciate the non-glamorous work that gets done many layers below them. I fear we do that too. We have to let the people below us in the org chart know that we value what they do, and the best way to do that is to do it with them, or for them, at least once," Nordy said as he shut off the lights and ushered them out of the dairy parlor.

As they approached the door of the house, Nordy held it open and said, "Well, hopefully your boots and gloves kept you from being too 'hands on' at this milking. Make sure you take your boots and overalls off before you step inside the house or Michelle and Stan will kill me."

Nordy ushered them all around the kitchen table. After washing up and changing out of his filthy overalls, he gave them the schedule for the rest of the day as he put coffee and tea on and served them. He opened the floor for questions about the milking process he had just demonstrated. The team had taken great notes and their questions were all good and filled in important gaps.

When the questions and eating had petered out, Nordy walked toward his room to change. Joanne, the General Counsel, followed him to his door and smiled with one final question. "Nordy, we have just one more question we all started wondering last night. Since your brother and sister-in-law gave up their weekend off for their neighbors, please tell us the neighbors are taking

advantage of it by going somewhere interesting
to do something fun."

"Well, they are going to an interesting place—
Germany. Unfortunately it is not for fun. They are
bringing their son's remains back home," Nordy
said as he closed his door.

Chapter 5
Colleagues Help Colleagues

After lunch, the rest of the team stayed around the dining room table to debrief from the morning milking operation and plan the next one. Nordy gave them their privacy by doing some chores outside and throwing a recipe in the crock-pot for dinner. By mid-afternoon, he broke up their meeting and let them know it was time to start again.

As the cows ambled in, the team met back in the dairy parlor. They pulled out a checklist of tasks with names assigned for each and started replicating the process they had witnessed that morning. Nordy stood in a corner silently watching. He had to force himself to stay quiet when they made minor mistakes that he knew they would eventually figure out. He did jump in when they made errors that presented a risk of injury to people or cows. Instead of just fixing the problem, however, he called "Time Out!" to make them all stop and have them figure out what they were doing wrong by asking questions.

Despite the fact that five people were doing the work that one person had done earlier that day, the milking and cleanup took more than twice as long as it had that morning. After the last box on their list was checked off, they all high-fived.

As they walked back to the house they saw a big brown Buick in the driveway. Nordy's brother and sister-in-law, Stan and Michelle, came by to meet them over dinner. Everyone introduced themselves as they met the couple in the kitchen. Stan and Michelle set the table while everyone else washed up. As they sat down for dinner, the team went out of their way to praise Stan and Michelle for their hospitality, especially the meal that welcomed them their first night.

The conversation soon turned to the neighbors that Michelle and Stan were helping. "Their son Kurt was wounded while on a patrol in Iraq about two weeks ago," Michelle explained. "He was flown to a military hospital in Germany and had several surgeries but passed away a few days after. Nordy was kind enough to arrange for them to fly to Germany to be with him at the hospital. Unfortunately they didn't make it in time to see him alive but at least they will be able to escort his remains back." She had to stop for a minute to wipe away tears.

"The sad irony is that Kurt always wanted to take his parents to Germany. He did a family tree project in high school and identified the little village in Germany where his ancestors had left to come to America. He was saving up to fly his parents over there to meet him in a few months when his tour was over." Michelle had to stop again and Nordy picked up, as tears now welled in the eyes of every team member.

"Because cows need milking seven days a week, fifty-two weeks a year, the saying goes that dairy farmers only get a day off when someone gets married or buried. Whenever one of those happens, it means their dairy-farming neighbors cover for them by milking twice as much that day. That's why Stan and Michelle are covering for them now."

They ended dinner with a toast and a moment of silence for Kurt. The rest of the team cleared the table and did the dishes while Nordy, Stan and Michelle caught up over coffee.

The next morning was the real test. The team did the milking entirely on their own while Nordy waited in the house, on-call in case he was needed. He watched nervously through the kitchen window as he prepared lunch. He had to draw upon all his patience and self-control not to go out to check several times. The first time was when the compressor that loudly ran the entire pumping system went out. The minutes it took them to restart it seemed like an eternity. The second time was when he saw a cow in the front yard staring at three executives trying to coax her back to the barn. When the milking passed the three-hour mark, he worried that something must have gone terribly wrong and was about to go out when he heard the compressor shut off again and the door open. The crew came in looking more tired, dirty and disheveled than he had ever seen. But they beamed as they gave him their report with a simple collective thumbs-up as they went to wash up for lunch.

As they sat down to eat, Nordy toasted the team for doing a milking on their own. "I won't lie," he started, "I almost ran out there to check several times. But I have enough confidence in you as a team that I didn't. And anyway, by setting this up so I could observe and respond immediately, I was giving you a learning environment where you could fail safely. You learn so much more when you fail and have to figure out what went wrong and how to fix it. The key for leaders is to find opportunities for their teams to fail in a way that won't be irreparable or unsafe. That is why this retreat made sense to me. Thank you for humoring me.

"And now, because you have succeeded as a team, here is your next surprise. Pack up because you are going to that fancy resort down the road for the rest of the trip as a reward. I'll cover the milking this afternoon and join you tomorrow night, as Stan will be back here the next morning."

COO Jerry then looked at the rest of his colleagues and stood. "Actually, with all due respect, we are not going to that resort. We decided to do something for Michelle and Stan, and Kurt and his parents instead. We've made all the arrangements. Michelle and Stan are going to the resort instead of us for the rest of our retreat. It will make up for the vacation they missed. A couple of us will go with you, Nordy, to take care of Kurt's family farm. The rest of us will stay here and do all the milking and chores."

Jerry then looked at Eva, who picked up the explanation. "We filled in our teams at work and posed a challenge to them. They figured out Kurt's family tree connections in Germany and the village he wanted to go to. They contacted the pastor in the church in that village to explain the situation. The pastor offered to hold a special memorial service for Kurt and his family. He guaranteed it would be full, as the village is a small but very tight-knit community. The team made all the arrangements to get Kurt and his parents to the village and to get them home. We all are pitching in to cover the costs."

Nora then jumped in to explain that part of the reason they were so long milking was because they were also doing conference calls with their teams from the sole landline phone in the dairy parlor. "I still have no idea how Lloyd figured out how to rig up an Internet connection from the dial-up," she closed with.

For the first time since that brutal staff meeting a few weeks ago where he had to sit and listen to all the blistering feedback on his leadership, Nordy was speechless.

With that, Joanne raised her glass and proposed a toast. "To Nordy, for showing us what leadership and teamwork look like. And to Stan, Michelle and Kurt, because we dairy-farming colleagues have to have each other's backs."

THE END

About the Author: As the Chief Operating Officer of the Consumer Financial Protection Bureau, **Victor Prince** led a division of 300 people. As a Bain & Company consultant, he helped clients across the US and Europe develop successful business strategies. His book, *Lead Inside the Box: How Smart Leaders Guide their Teams to Exceptional Results* was named a Top 20 Leadership Book of the Year for 2016. Today, Victor is a consultant and speaker who teaches strategy and leadership skills to clients around the world. Learn more at www.victorprince.com.